YES YOU CAN SERIES

THE SEXY MEDIUM'S LOVE AND LUST SPELLS

Maria D' Andrea

YES YOU CAN SERIES

THE SEXY MEDIUM'S LOVE AND LUST SPELLS

By Maria D'Andrea, MsD, D.D., DRH

INNER LIGHT/GLOBAL COMMUNICATIONS

YES YOU CAN SERIES

The Sexy Medium's Love and Lust Spells

By Maria D'Andrea,MsD, D.D., DRH

© 2016 Maria D'Andrea

Published by Timothy Green Beckley

DBA Inner Light/Global Communications - All Rights Reserved

Printed in the United States of America

Non-Fiction

Timothy Green Beckley: Editorial Director

Carol Ann Rodriguez: Publishers Assistant

Sean Casteel: Editor

Associate Editor & Graphics: Tim R. Swartz

William Kern: Associate Editor

Email: mrufo8@hotmail.com

www.ConspiracyJournal.Com

CONTENTS

DEDICATION

To both of my magickal sons:

Rob D'Andrea and Rick Holecek

Both of my sons are always there for me and inspiring me. They have their own philosophies, are explorers of life, selfless and great communicators. I value their opinions, respect them and truly hold them in very high esteem. I feel truly blessed that they came into this Realm to be with me.

FOREWORD

By Rick Holecek

YOU are looking for a relationship. Whether it is the romantic, long-term storybook type, the down and dirty lusty type, or a combination of both, this book can help. You don't need to consider yourself spiritually strong to make it work, though it wouldn't hurt. All you have to do is follow the step-by-step instructions found in this book.

I am an engineer, by nature and by training, but Maria taught me how to pay attention to my spiritual gifts also. Through her guidance, I was able to learn how to do some amazing things that most engineers wouldn't dream of. She taught me how to meditate; how to read others and help them grow; and how to manifest things that I need in my life, including love. Granted, I had an unfair advantage. I am her son.

What you will love about this book is that you don't need to have years of training. Maria has a huge library of books and an amazing wealth of knowledge on which she draws. She saves you all those years of research by summarizing it here in this book. The funniest part is that a lot of what she writes down is through automatic writing (allowing spirit to use her body to write) so you won't find it anywhere else. Some of this will be "Hot off the Universal Press," so to speak.

Some of what she taught me about bringing in romance or love worked so well that my friends took notice and asked me to put them in touch with her. But be aware of what you are really asking for because you will likely get exactly what you are looking for. I once manifested two women in my life. Together they had everything on my list, but neither one would make me happy. I decided to refine my manifesting to one person that was European, attractive and emotional. The person I met next was European, very attractive and very over-emotional. The lesson to the story is "Watch what you ask for!" I refined my manifesting more and I am now happily married with two fantastic kids and a wonderful life.

Keep positive and know that these techniques work as long as you are not trying to overcome another person's free will.
Enjoy!

THE MAGICK OF LOVE AND LUST

IT is time to consciously work with having a joyful life. This includes, of course, love and lust. Love is the strongest and most powerful force in the universe.

Don't forget that there are several types of love. The obvious one is a romantic relationship. However, there is also the love of friends, children, parents, family, pets (we don't have to work on them, they just love us), to name just a few.

The formulae in my books are very ancient and powerful or are my original ones developed after years of being a shaman, occultist, professional psychic, working with magick and other modalities. Some magickal formulae are so ancient that they don't even have names, so I named them.

You can bring in a new love or an old one back. You can improve on the relationship you have. The spells bring in the contact but they don't force the situation to be forever. Whether you stay together or not, that is free will. We don't control in a negative way. We can also move someone out of our lives without harming them.

WE ONLY DO POSITIVE WORK. If you attract someone in a negative way, not only will it not last, but if it does, it can be dangerous and it will be very difficult to get rid of the intended person.

Example: I had a client come to me years ago for help. She was dating a gentleman for several years and was tired of waiting for him to want to get married.

I checked out the situation psychically for myself before deciding if I should help or not. I had a very bad feeling about the situation and told her it was a bad idea and that it wouldn't turn out well. I also told her she should move on to a new relationship immediately.

Of course, she didn't want to hear that. I couldn't help her ethically, so she went to someone else.

She was married to her intended gentleman about three years later. Everything was fine. They were happy for about a year. I received a call from her soon after that time.

It seemed that when her husband was growing up, his father was a wife beater. He wasn't aware he had that tendency until he was married for a while. She was not only being hit, she was devastated emotionally.

She asked me if I could help, but by then she had already had very bad experiences that could have been avoided. I also advised her to move out, which she did. When she first dated him, he was loving, like her.

There is the Law of "Like attracts Like." It comes into play in our everyday lives. Have you noticed when you look at people in groups, they seem to have some of the same qualities?

If someone is positive and has a good outlook on life, that person will feel uncomfortable in a group of people who are negative and look at only problems instead of solutions. Of course, the same holds if someone is negative: they will feel uncomfortable with positive people.

Love and lust actually go together in a love relationship. If you feel love for a person but you don't have chemistry, it will not last long term. The same holds true if you feel attracted to a person but do not love them; it will not last. They go together. We are spirit but we live in a physical body. We need both.

I do not mean to say that you cannot have just one aspect and still be happy. There is nothing wrong with that. You simply need to be consciously aware. The two are not the same.

Love is an emotional feeling and lust is chemistry manifesting as an attraction.

Short term is one thing, long term would need both. There are no good or bad decisions, only your decision. Each situation is different. Decide accordingly what you feel is best for you.

*** Important: Understanding the soul level attraction. Lust is a physical reaction/alchemy. You feel a spiritual connection and are picking it up as a physical outward manifestation of energy. It is not only physical. The vibration is on a soul level connection. Remember, the vibration is physical but comes after the soul connection.

When you utilize magick, you have to have a definite intent. That could be a specific person or someone you haven't met yet. It could be a friend, love interest or family.

You also have to have focus and exert will power when you are being a practitioner. (Or a Light Worker or any other name you may go by.)

Knowledge is always the Key. It is the Power. Know what you are doing before you start. Make sure it is what your heart desires.

Prepare by having everything ready before you begin.

Expect it to work. If you don't think it will, it definitely will not. You will cancel yourself out. Make sure you approach magick with reverence and seriousness.

Our ultimate goal is for you and a romantic partner or friend to both have a happy life. So open your heart.

Remember that you are working with powerful love energies. We always work from the heart and work toward both people being happy.

The following chapters will give you choices of how to work with the energies of the universe to achieve your goals in a positive way.

LOVE ATTRACTION SPELLS

THERE are a few basics. We never focus our intent on any particular person without adding this or better. If we do not have a specific person in mind, instead, we say: <u>my partner</u> or <u>focus on the type of person you are manifesting.</u>

There are specific deities connected to Love that we can call on for help. We don't need to necessarily, but, if we choose that method, we need to know some of the correct ones for love and friendship.

Know that we bring the person in to make contact. We do not make the person stay with us (that is negative, because we do not go against free will).

When we utilize oils, gemstones or herbs, we don't need to believe in them. They work vibrationally whether we believe in them or not.

You cannot do a formula/spell and question if it will work because then it won't. It's a self-fulfilling prophecy. Talismans and sigils work by a vibration that is connected on the ethers to a specific deity or situation. With either ancient spells or my original formulae, I know after many years of work and study that the cause will have the same effect each time. So it is with this book of love and lust and friendship.

Partial List To Add On As Options:

<u>Some Male Deities:</u> Eros, Cupid, Adonis, Woden, Osiris

THE SEXY MEDIUM'S LOVE AND LUST SPELLS

<u>Some Female Deities:</u> Venus, Diane, Aphrodite, Frey, Bridget

<u>Main Planet Ruler:</u> Venus

<u>Venus Connects To</u>: Friday, Copper, Friends, Love, Travel, Marriage, Lust. The color is green.

<u>Sun:</u> This day is related to Sunday. It is for all forms of Success and can connect to any deities. Color is gold or yellow.

<u>Direction:</u> Best is facing the South or West (South is best for Lust).

<u>Chakra:</u> Polarity Chakra, orange color.

<u>Colors:</u> Red (will, love, sex appeal, strength, courage), Pink (love), Green (love), Gold (Universal Love), Orange (for lust).

<u>Stones:</u> Pearl (Any white stone for friendship), Rhodonite (love), Diamond (purity, joy, happy life), Emerald (success in heart matters), Sardonyx (marriage), Topaz (love, friendship, fidelity), Balas Ruby (marital bliss), Onyx (marital love, devotion), Bohemian Topaz (fidelity), Peridot (friendship).

<u>Best color to attract women:</u> Red

<u>Best color to attract men:</u> Red or Pink

RITUAL TO BRING IN LOVE

Use a pink piece of material or pink handkerchief.

In the center put a few drops of Success or Love oil.

Add together on the cloth:

1-The name of the person that you want to come into your life.

Or

If you don't have a specific person in mind, then write My Right Partner. Add This or Better. Write this on white paper with black ink.

2-A rose quartz stone (size doesn't matter)

3-A rhodocrosite stone

4-Few pieces of the violet flower

Tie the cloth with everything in it closed with 5 knots.

Light a pink 7 Day Candle and hold the pouch you just made over it.

Focus on your intent.

Call in with authority the name of Venus:

Oh, Venus of the Loving Flame,

Your feminine energies are requested today,

Fire and Water,

Air and Earth,

Bring to me my mate on Earth.

Bring <u>(state his / her name)</u> in a Positive Way,

Bless me with this, as I now say.

From dawn 'till dusk,

From dusk 'till dawn,

Work your magick,

One hundred strong.

So Mote It Be!

Let the candle burn to the socket. Throw away any wax that is left outside of your home.

Place the pouch under your bed and leave it there.

Start this on a Friday. Each Friday hold the pouch in your hands and repeat the incantation with focus. Then place it back under the bed.

Expect it to come. Do this until your desire comes in.

MAGNETIC POWER TO ATTRACT MEN

Blend the following oils and wear a drop or two daily (especially before you go out).

Ambergris - Jasmine - Lavender

Focus on your intent as you put this on your heart and wrists. Remember to smile.

MAGNETIC POWER TO ATTRACT WOMEN

Blend the following oils together. Wear the oil each day and before being around women. Place a drop in the palm of your hand. One drop goes on your throat and one on your heart.

Musk - Civet (a little) - Bay (a little)

Focus on your intent when putting this on. Remember to smile.

FIDELITY IN LOVE

Carry a Bohemian Topaz stone at all times. Give one to your loved one to carry in the same way.

EXCITEMENT OF LOVE

Incantation:

Hear me, Deities of Love! Hear me Hera and Osiris! Thou spirits of Venus! I desire to excite love and passion in the heart of (fill in the name of the person. If there is no specific person, say my Right

Partner). Work your magick so my love is returned a hundredfold. Work this for me if it is positive and good for all!

I conjure this command thus!

Through Isten and Hathor! So Mote It Be!

The best day to do this is on a Friday or a Sunday.

PASSION

Mix:

½ oz. Orris Root Powder

½ oz. Anise Seed

¼ oz. saltpeter

½ oz. dried Lavender

4 oz. Rose Powder

½ oz. dried Red Clover

Use this as herbal incense. Burn self-igniting charcoal until it is burning strongly, then sprinkle the blend over it. Concentrate on your desire. On a white paper, using red ink, write the name of the person five times. Then use a match to light it and burn it to ashes in a dish while holding the dish over the incense. When you have done this and all is turned into ashes, go outside and throw it all to the wind.

Do this for seven days. Use two to three drops of Love Oil on your heart to achieve the results. (If female, you can substitute Rose Oil, if you are male, you can substitute Musk Oil.)

NEW LOVER

Get the herb called Couch Grass. Sprinkle a little under your mattress to attract a new lover.

Works in a short time, so keep an eye out.

SPELL OF LOVE

Anoint a red candle with Love Oil or Rose Oil. Say this incantation for five nights in a row.

Repeat three times in a row:

I am possessed by love that is burning for (name) and

I want (name) to have the same burning love for me and me only.

Let this come from spirit and enter (name).

(Name) must feel the same feeling as I feel.

Spirit of the Air and Fire let (name) burn for me

As long as it is for the good of us both.

So Be It.

LOVE VIBRATIONS

Burn a red candle every night until the candle is out. Focus on your intent for five minutes at a time. Concentrate on the person that you want (or say My Right Partner) and say:

(Fill in the name) is the one I want, through Divine Power,

In a Perfect Way, for now and forever.

As this light burns, so does (his or her name) burn for me,

And only I can fulfill this desire.

So Mote It Be.

CANDLE CHART

Any brand you buy will work for you. It doesn't matter if it's expensive or not because they all work the same vibrationally.

If you aren't sure which to use or you are working on love and friendship at the same time, with the same person, then use white. White is an all-purpose color.

The candles with the shapes are good for helping you to keep your focus on your intent. See which resonate with you at the time. Any spells in my book dealing with candle colors can be substituted with one of the following on this chart.

Try different methods to see which suits you best at the time.

For any candle magick, you have color correlations to be aware of.

CANDLE SPELL ENHANCERS

Type	Purpose	Color
Cat	Love	Red
Image (Shaped as person)	Love	Red
	Friends	Pink
Seven Knob	Wishes	Multi
Witch	Love	Red
Double Action	Love, Sex, Energy	Black & Red
Triple Action	Love, Blessing, Home harmony	Red, White, Blue
Triple Action	Love, Blessing, Luck	Red, White, Green

Seven Day candles stay lit for seven consecutive days. Sometimes they last a little shorter or longer. That is fine. Some are "pull out" candles and can be taken out of their glass. Some can't.

MEDICINE BAG FOR LOVE ATTRACTION

Make sure you focus on your intent during the whole process.

Use a red bag or pouch or simply sew one. Add the following ingredients into the bag:

¼ tsp. Couch Grass

¼ tsp. Linden Flowers

7 Rose Buds

2 Tonka Beans

¼ tsp. Vervain

¼ tsp. Lavender

1/8 tsp. Attraction Powder

Tie the bag closed with three knots.

Place two or three drops only of Love Oil or Rose Oil in the palm of your hands and rub the bag between them.

Concentrate on the name of the person you want (add- *or better-* so we don't limit it or do something negative by accident). Visualize how you want the person (marriage, date, friend, etc.). Remember to <u>say</u>:

In A Perfect Way.

Carry this medicine bag with you at all times until the results you want come in.

<u>Client's Story</u>

I had a wonderful student who really wanted a love relationship. Unfortunately he worked so many hours that he didn't get out much.

He was very frustrated. He felt he had so much to give and he loved children.

He thought about how it didn't look too good for him. The few women he met were more interested in his money and he didn't have much in common with them.

We talked about his best option with the formulae.

He also wanted to meet someone who was spiritual. Not that she had to go to church, although he went on and off, but that she had a spiritual outlook and ethics.

So he did the Medicine Bag formulae.

It was a few months later, but he kept extremely focused on his intent and on expecting it to come in. He trusted that it works no matter how long it takes. He knew it was *when* it comes, not *if* it comes.

He was coming out of his building on the elevator, and, every day, no matter what time he left, there was the same woman. They started to talk about how funny that was. He asked her out for coffee a short while after and they ended up going out. She was just what he was manifesting. Funny how it works . . .

LOVE – VERY POWERFUL

During the night of the new moon, concentrate on what you desire. Write this down on a piece of paper and add the name of the one you desire on it. If you don't have a specific person, write – My Perfect Partner. Use red ink on white paper. (Dove's Blood ink is best on *parchment paper.) Fold the paper three times folding from top down.* Place an emerald stone next to it. Burn the paper in an ashtray or something non-flammable and focus strongly on what you want –   NOW and in a Perfect Way.

When it is all ashes (you may have to relight it), throw it outside to the wind.

Take the emerald and carry it with you until you get your results.

FRIENDSHIPS ARE SACRED

The reason I say friendships are sacred is because those are the people we tell our innermost secrets to, have fun with, play sports or go to games with, have common ground with, depend on for help or advice, and can trust.

Sometimes we outgrow friendships. If you had a friend for 90 years and for the last two they are miserable and negative, you might be waiting for them to return to their former self. If they do not, you need to move on in a positive way. You don't wish them anything bad, you simply want to move on.

Sometimes it can be that you have moved to more knowledge, higher spiritual levels, gained different interests through time, and they have not. You still need to move on and meet people who fit your new self in a positive way.

And at times we have wonderful friends and just wish to heighten what we have.

Don't forget, if you relocate, your friends might be wonderful, but you will look for new friends in your new area. (It could be out of state, out of the country or maybe the next town.)

There are several formulae you can use depending on the intent you are working on. Use them wisely.

ATTRACT NEW FRIENDS

Wear Sweet Pea and rub a little lemon on your wrists each day. After they come in, it is up to you to keep it going naturally.

LEMON WISH FOR FRIENDSHIP

Take a whole lemon and make sure there are no cuts or bruises on it.

Tie a pink ribbon on it, tying it around four times. Focus your intent on new friendships coming into your life.

Wrap it in pink cloth. Tie it with pink thread, using three knots, to keep it closed.

Hold either palm over the lemon, think of energy flowing from your palm into the lemon, and <u>say</u>:

New friendships now come unto me,

Come by land or air or sea,

I am open to the new,

Friendships come if you are true.

As friends come in,

A friend I'll be,

My heart is open,

For all to see,

As I will,

So Mote It Be!

Take the lemon and throw it into any body of water as far as you can. Make sure you are friendly, open and smiling as you do this. It is safe to be open.

FRIENDSHIPS THROUGH NATURE

When you want to attract new friends or connect better with the ones you have, wear the color pink. With men, this can be any shade, such as a light pastel that is almost white.

Also wear something made of copper.

WISHES FULFILLED

This will work for any wish. However, it is wonderful for friendships. Either improving the ones you have or gaining new ones.

Get the herb known as Grains Of Paradise. Hold some in your hands and focus on your intent. Then throw them to the wind a little at a time in the four directions.

Start with the east and end up in the west. Then walk away.

LUCK IN FRIENDSHIPS

The Aloe plant has numerous uses. One reliable usage is to hang the plant or part of it over any entry into your home to attract friendship to you.

LUCK IN NEW FRIENDSHIPS

Carry a piece of the wood rose with you as you focus on new friendships coming to you.

Keep a positive attitude and remember to smile. After all, if someone looks angry or upset, would you want to be their friend?

We are working with both realities. Spiritual and physical.

LASTING FRIENDSHIPS OF THE FAIRIES

Carry a pouch/bag that is either white or pink.

In it, place:

A small piece of Carnelian. Some petals of a rose. Put a few drops of oil on the pouch (Men, put Musk Oil/Women, put Rose Oil)

Tie the pouch closed with three knots. Use a pink candle of any size. Light the candle.

Hold the pouch over it and <u>say with intent and sincerity</u>:

Candle, candle burning bright,

Bring to me my friendships Right.

I now call upon the fairy realm,

Bring me friendships that will last.

From brightest day,

To evening's dusk,

I will be faithful,

I know I must.

And as the fire goes out today,

Its energies I use to pay.

Payment given free and safe.

From me to you on this brightest day.

So Mote It Be!

Keep the pouch with you at all times. Let the candle burn out by itself to the bottom. Then throw it anywhere outside your home.

UN-HEXING BY FIRE

If you feel you are not gaining or having positive friends because someone wishes you not to do well, then this will help you. Keep a positive attitude for it to work.

Start it on a Wednesday. In a purple bag, add a little of each:

Dandelion

Rosemary

Clove

Basil

Mistletoe

Witch Grass

Vanilla Bean

Or put small drops of Vanilla Oil on the bag. Carry it with you at all times. Sleep with the bag near you.

CIRCLE OF FRIENDS

Friends are very important. We gain and give advice, cheer each other up, have someone to vent to, and have a helping hand, among other attributes.

If you have some friends who are open to spiritually working together, then do the following:

1 - Form a circle and hold hands to complete the circle.

2 - One person needs to be the head (YOU – in a positive way).

3 - Do a short verbal Prayer for Protection of your choosing. It can be short, such as <u>saying</u>: Divine Power Protect us in this circle until we are done.

4 - Next, have each person say what they would like to have everyone focus on to help them. Such as: improving one's health, a better car, a happy relationship, a better job, credit for their work, a raise, accomplishing something, etc.

5 - Next, have everyone focus for a few seconds on the successful desired outcome for the person, then move on to the next person and repeat the process.

6 - After everyone has finished, focus on positive energy flowing in the circle going toward the right, through one hand to the next, completing the circle. Keep it going until you (as the leader) feel it is time to stop. Now <u>say</u>: We now stop sending the energy flow.

7 – <u>Say</u>: **We thank you, Divine Power, and each other for this positive connection.**

8 - Still holding hands, as a closing, <u>Say as a command</u>: **May this circle be open but not broken.**

9 - Let go of each other's hands at this point and go about your daily business (or have everyone stay for coffee/tea).

   You can do this once or once in a while to keep a positive connection.

SECRETS OF LUST POTIONS

I would like to tell you it's also love, but in reality . . . it isn't.

Now, don't misunderstand me. It doesn't mean there isn't love there or that love won't follow, but these potions are on an aphrodisiac level. So be aware.

Love potions are blends which have a high rate of having amorous results when the person drinks it or blends various items from nature.

Part of the magick of love/lust potions is that there is power in your thought, in the Word.

Remember, we only do positive. If for any reason, in a love spell or lust potion, if it isn't good for both parties, it will cancel itself out.

Focus on your intent as you blend the formulae and decide what you want as a result before you start. This links the petitioner with the universal mind forces and telepathically sets off a trigger in the mind of the person you desire.

When your focus is intent as you are blending, you are activating the energy forces to work as a magnet culminating in the outcome you set forth.

I would like to tell you to use these with caution, but if you are reading this chapter, do I really need to add that?

TIGER LUST – For Men

(Better then Viagra and doesn't have bad side effects.)

This potion is utilized for the purpose of stamina in the male. Stimulator.

Fill ¾ of an 8 oz. glass with Guinea Stout

Add 3 teaspoons sweet condensed milk

1 raw egg

Beat together. Drink it immediately. It is taken thirty to forty-five minutes before becoming intimate. (Afterward, you can repeat . . .)

EYE OF THE GIANT – For Men

(Another one that is better than Viagra and doesn't have bad side effects.)

This is for non-alcoholic users. Same results on a power level as Tiger Lust.

Fill ¾ of an 8 oz. glass with milk

1 banana

1 raw egg

3 teaspoons honey (or to taste)

A few raisins (optional)

Blend these ingredients together. Drink immediately. To be taken thirty to forty-five minutes prior to intimacy.

This can be drunk before and after if you want to reproduce the results.

SENSUAL VIBRATION

Burn Rose Incense in the room when you want a sensual mood. Your partner will react to the scent.

LUST OF THE GODS

Burn Vanilla Incense and wear two to three drops of Vanilla Oil on your throat and Third Eye. Put one drop in your palm with focus. Rub your palms together.

DRAGON WINE

Boil the following ingredients:

16 oz. red wine

Five cinnamon sticks

Drink while it is still warm.

WINE OF THE SWORD

Bring the following ingredients to a boil:

16 oz. red wine

A few cloves

Drink this while still warm.

ELFIN SPIRITS

1/5 Vodka – pour into a jar or bottle.

Bring the following to a boil: 1 two oz. jar of instant coffee, 1 vanilla bean, 1 small container of sesame seeds, 1 lb. sugar, Add to the vodka.

Note: *** There are lust potions sold commercially, though they don't advertise them as aphrodisiacs. ***

34

They were used in old lust potions or as part of the ingredients. So here is a list (why reinvent the wheel?):

Sloe Gin: A liqueur from the sloe berry. Also called blackthorn. Was added to love/lust potions.

May Wine: This is a sweet white wine, flavored with woodruff.

Advokaat: An egg and brandy liqueur.

Drambuie: It has a base of Scotch malt whiskey. Also contains spices and honey.

Metaxa: Greek resinous sweet, dark liqueur. Has a brandy base.

Vermouth: This wine contains most of the herbs and the barks used in the old love potions. One of the ingredients is called Wermut, meaning "essence of man," thus the name Vermouth. Not too subtle . . .

ROAD TO PARADISE

Part of any good romantic relationship is chemistry. You need to feel that fire. You have to have the emotions to go with it. Nonetheless, passion has to do with chemistry between two people.

You get that sizzling feeling, that electricity when you are around your special person.

Do the following to get results:

In a red bag (pouch/mojo bag/medicine bag/conjure bag – just thought I'd give you a few other names for it) place the following:

Adam and Eve root, a small piece of copper, Rhodocrosite – pink stone, Pink Attraction Powder.

Close the bag with five knots. Put a drop of Success Oil on the bag and focus on what you're intent is; feel the emotions you are going to feel; expect it to manifest.

Still holding the bag, place it between your palms and verbally, with sincerity, <u>say</u>:

Body to body,

Heart to heart,

As we do so,

We are one.

Then carry the bag with you at all times. When you sleep, place it close to your bed.

***Remember, we only do positive, so this will work as long as it is positive for both of you.

<u>GOBLIN JUICE</u>

This is very good to use as a party punch. Not as powerful as those mentioned prior. After all, it is meant for a party. *** Do not let children drink it.**

Add these ingredients together:

1/5 rum, 1/5 Vodka, 1 large can of pineapple-grapefruit drink, 1 small can of frozen orange juice, (Diluted as instructed on the container), 4 oz. Grenadine

Serve this with ice and have fun.

My student's husband:

One of my students was coming for psychic/metaphysical (positive occult) classes for years. Her husband was a very nice gentleman and was very supportive of her but he personally didn't have any interest in the subjects. Which was fine. He would sit in my living room and watch TV or read.

They were going to have a BBQ party the following week and she decided to make this punch.

He called me the next day (which had never happened before) and said that his in-laws have always disliked him. They were married for over 20 years and that still had never changed.

His in-laws had the punch and he said that not only were they friendly toward him for the first time, but they were in a "friendly" mood and went home early.

He said he doesn't care what I teach her, he will always come and bring her to the classes happily.

You can't make this stuff up . . .

SPIRITUAL ATTRACTION BATHS

A spiritual bath, also called an immersion bath, is one in which you are immersing yourself in the water to attract a situation or to do a banishing with specific intents/goals. In this case, it's lust. Come on, you know it's a part of nature . . .

This technique is nothing new. They have utilized these baths since ancient times and the only difference now is that we get to use a bathtub. That makes it more convenient, right?

You add different herbs or other tools of nature to the bath to change the water's vibration to match your intent. You never add soap or anything else at this time because the ritual will not work then. You would be adding a different vibration (soap) then what your intent would be and that would cancel it out.

There should be enough water so you can duck under for a second to have the water cover you completely.

Next, focus on something positive for at least 15 minutes. It can be longer, but not a shorter time or the vibration will not mesh with your aura/energy field thoroughly enough.

You can focus on love and/or lust and the positive feelings that come with them. You can also focus on prayer, a vacation you had fun on in the past, a wonderful situation from your past, or a positive, happy event in the future that you are looking forward to. Or even a wonderful daydream. As long as it is positive, it works.

If you think of something negative during this time (because we are human), immediately say the word "cancel" and change it to a positive thought instead.

You can pick one ingredient or combine some to add to the water as long as they have the same purpose. For example, love and lust, because they can work together.

When dealing with some of the herbs, it is easier to make them into a tea first. Otherwise, you will have loose herbs floating all over your tub and it will be annoying to clean out when you are finished. Why make it harder? You would take a cup and a half of water and add a tablespoon of the herb. Let it boil on low for 20 minutes.

Next, strain the water and throw the herbs out. Add the herbal water to the bath water. You can make more of this "tea" to add, but this amount will do nicely, since it's vibrational.

You probably have some of the ingredients with your cooking herbs in the kitchen. Some ingredients might be found at a park, backyard, street and other places.

If you are dealing with a bean, as an example, just add the whole bean into the water. Directly from nature is a great thing. Of course, just wash it off first of dirt or debris.

Partial list of Ingredients:

Love: Rose

Adam and Eve Root

Dill (again, probably in your kitchen)

Sweet pea

Clove

Lotus

Pistachio (just throw the whole nut into the water)

Lust: Celery

Lucky Hand

Nutmeg

Caraway

Cinnamon (you can use the cinnamon stick)

Vervain

Friendship: Lemon

Passion flower

Daffodil

Rose

Oak

Poppy

Family: I'm adding family because of love, harmony and balance.

Basil

Lilac

Gardenia

Rose

When you are finished with your spiritual bath, try to air dry. If you can't (we have to get to work, among other reasons), then towel dry. Stay focused on your goal and keep an eye out for it coming in.

OUR SECRET LANGUAGES

THERE are many little things we do and can do that are not obvious but move us forward in our romantic lives. Some we already do consciously and some not. Recognize these small things and work with them to improve your life.

FLOWERS OF FUN

Make an impression with flowers and know some of their meanings to get your point across. And also be aware for times when you receive them.

<u>Rose colors:</u>   Red   - romance, passion in love, beauty, courage

Pink - admiration, grace, gratitude

White - new starts, purity, youthfulness, respect, happy (Bridal)

Yellow – happiness, friendship, jealousy, new starts

Orange – excitement, desire, enthusiasm

Peach - appreciation, gratitude, desire, modesty

Lavender – love at first sight

These colors also hold for other flowers.

FLIRTATION AS AN ART

Flirting has been a basic ability since time began. We simply have a conscious way to work with these "hints."

It is also about making contact with someone who is a romantic potential and about making that person and yourself feel good.

Remember to only do what you honestly feel. If you don't smile normally and it says you should, do so only if it is truly in your nature. We are not trying to give anyone misdirection about who we really are. It wouldn't be fair to either of you. Stay true to yourself.

You can flirt to meet someone new or when on a date or with someone you are married to. After all, being in a relationship already doesn't mean we shouldn't make it fun and exciting.

Here are some <u>fun techniques:</u>

      1 - If you see someone at a distance, such as across a room at a party, at the library, dance club, you get the point . . . You do the <u>Five Second Rule</u>. The rule is that you smile (you can smile before you turn your head to look so you aren't as obvious), look into the eyes of the person you are interested in, and count to five seconds. It will seem like a very long time, because normally we don't take as long. Then look away and you don't need to look back again. If you are a lady and he's at all interested, he will come over. (He would not be interested, as an example, if he was married or in a relationship.) If you are a gentleman and the lady looked back, then, after the five, walk over to her.

If someone was not interested, as in the examples given previously, they would not return the gaze either. Good, you just did a shortcut and can move on to another interesting person more quickly.

2 - Feelings are important, so compliment the person on something real. Flattery actually makes both of you happy. Think about the last time you complimented a friend and how good you felt. It can be about their eyes,

their cologne, shirt, or it can be that the person said something interesting. He/she will feel good toward you because you saw something in him/her that is special. Being Real is Important!

3 - Be genuinely interested and listen more than you talk. If you are interested . . . You are interested, right? Of course you are, because you are talking to someone and here in the first place. You would genuinely be interested in what they like to do or whatever they are speaking about because it has meaning to them. (It also lets you know how compatible you are.) Then don't change the subject right away. Ask questions about what they just said. Example: if they talked about a vacation they went on years ago, ask what they liked the most about it, how long they were there, etc. It shows an interest in them and confirms that you were paying attention to them. They will feel more appreciated and comfortable around you.

4 - While you are talking, make sure you smile! Even before you first speak to someone new, if you are smiling talking to a friend, you are more approachable – men and women. While you are talking (and smiling, of course), touch the person on the arm for a quick second. If you are making a point in the conversation, that's a good time. Don't do more than a second, because it can be misread by men as too clingy/overly friendly/sexual and women can misread it as a man being too aggressive/sexual/intimidating.

Remember, flirting should be fun. Be a love magnet.

VIBRATIONAL STONES OF POWER

STONES have their own vibrational energies. You don't have to believe in them for them to work for you. They have been utilized since ancient times and the knowledge is passed down to us through shamans, magi, angels, Light Workers and other spiritual beings. We do get information from other realms.

Stones have more than one purpose. However, we are only focused on the love, lust and friendship intents in this book. Fun and laughter are always good ideas.

Use the stones consciously to attract to you what you are manifesting in a positive way.

You can carry them within three feet of your body to attract your intent to you and sometimes you give the stone to someone else (I will let you know when to do this). You can always give a stone as a gift or give it in jewelry form. You can also put them in a pouch, wallet, pocketbook or pocket.

Moonstone – Wrap two stones separately in yellow cloths. Carry one and give the other to your romantic partner. This is to promote fidelity.

Amazonite – Attracts universal love and smooth's emotional upsets.

Green Aventurine – Creativity and imagination (you know you can use that, right?), luck and success.

Amethyst – Love, protection, calming and motivation.

THE SEXY MEDIUM'S LOVE AND LUST SPELLS

Dalmatian Jasper – Relationships of any type. (Including family.)

Green Obsidian – Goddess nature, nurturing and love.

Black Onyx – Releasing the past, which helps you to move on and break patterns that are holding you back.

Carnelian - Sexuality, motivation, trust and success.

Blue Calcedony – Harmony, happiness, emotional stabilizer.

Jade – Friendship, love, tranquility and luck.

Blue Quartz – Self-discipline and communication.

Mangano Calcite – Emotional healing, love and success.

Blue Calcite – Communication (you know, we can all use that) and clearer thinking.

Labradorite – Change, insight, truth, faith and new ideas.

Bronzite – Helps with decisions and clears confusion.

Moss Agate – New beginnings, harmony and releases stress and fear.

Bloodstone – Luck and victory.

Angelite – Contact angels and positive spirits to come to your aid. Faith, compassion and forgiveness (at times, we need to forgive ourselves or/and others to be able to move on).

Tangerine Quartz – Law of Attraction, relationships and sexual energy.

Blue Sapphire – Truth, commitment and loyalty.

Rhodocrosite – Opens the heart and lifts your mood.

Amphibole – Vitality.

<u>Pink Tourmaline</u> – Reconciliation, understanding, listening, emotionally calming, relationships and love.

<u>Black Tourmaline</u> – Understanding and self-confidence.

<u>Yellow Obsidian</u> – Love relationships, self-esteem and lifts your mood.

<u>Sunstone</u> – Luck, empowerment, independence and positive outlook.

<u>Emerald</u> – Domestic happiness, unconditional love, loyalty, friendship and unity.

<u>Fire Agate</u> – Passion and taking action.

<u>Garnet</u> – Passion, devotion, balancing, hope, love, sexuality and removes inhibitions.

<u>Lodestone</u> – Attracting and manifesting. (The lodestones come in pairs. Make sure that is how you get them.)

Always use them wisely.

OUR ANCESTRAL TOOLS

YOU know our ancestors were loving, sexual beings. How else would we get here???

They understood the electrical and magnetic influences around them. They utilized the tools of nature. They not only wanted to be lucky in friendships, love and lust but also to have laughter and joy in their lives.

Our ancestors utilized various tools in their environment. We can incorporate many of them today and work with them to bring about a positive outcome.

They also became a love magnet. Being aware of who you are (not conceited but self-aware) and your value, loving, being truthful, and knowing what you have to give is irresistible. Others will sense these traits and a loving nature emanating from you and will be drawn to you. As long as your traits are real, of course.

We have to respect our ancestors (people sometimes don't realize this includes parents who have passed on) and send them love energies as a thank you for all their help and for being connected to us.

CONCH SHELLS

These shells in nature can be found on beaches for us to use. You can also find them at some craft stores, hobby shops and other places.

Get a conch shell. Conch shells represent emotional communication. Take the shell and, using black ink or paint, write the name of the person you are manifesting into your life. If you don't have a specific person, write "My Right Partner." Also (anywhere on the shell) draw two hearts connecting. Then write your name on the shell, too.

Write what you are manifesting: freedom from a relationship (that happens), romantic relationship and lust, love, friendship, harmony, fun, commitment or whatever you decide.

Also write anywhere on it:

Through Divine Power

In A Perfect Way

This Or Better

We do this so we don't accidentally cause harm to ourselves or others.

Go to a body of water: ocean, lake, stream or any water.

Hold the conch shell between your hands and focus on what your intent/purpose is.

Call on Neptune, the God of the Seas (doesn't matter what body of water you use – water is water) to come to your aid and help you to manifest your intent in a positive way.

Then throw the shell into the water.

Thank Neptune for his help.

Turn around and walk away, knowing it is done. Do NOT look back. (If you look back, you just cancelled the spell and will have to start from scratch.)

TREE OF LOVE

Before you look for your special manifesting tree, decide on exactly what your intent is. Focus on it and make sure you think of all the details. What type of relationship is it? How do you want it to be? Make sure you think of both of you being happy (not just you . . .).

1 - Now, go to find a tree. It can be in the park, backyard, woods or any other place.

2 - Find an oak tree, peach tree, pine tree or apple tree. If they are not available near you, then use any tree, but these are best energetically for your purpose.

3 - Go up to it and touch it. Mentally ask this tree if it is willing to work with you. Give it a second and see how you feel. If you feel "off" or edgy or some form that doesn't feel good, then thank the tree (mentally or verbally) and find another tree. Sometimes they don't work with us for a variety of reasons, including that they might be sick. If you get a good feeling or no feeling at all/neutral, then you have permission from the tree to work with it.

4 -Touch the tree. At this point, remember that we do not need to be obvious to other people around us. We still do things "underground." Why be visible with spiritual work? So . . . you can lean on the tree with your hand (after all, you are just leaning), you can sit with your back leaning on the tree, stand with your back leaning on the tree or any other way.

5 - Now focus on "telling" (verbal or non-verbal) the tree exactly what your intent is. Give all the details you can think of. Remember to think of it as – this or better. Now visualize the outcome strongly. You can "see" it in color or black and white. It doesn't make a difference. The intent and focus does. Now, send the picture mentally into the tree.

6 - Thank the tree for helping you. Know that it is now done. Trust it to work. Expect it!

7 - Walk away.

SYMPATHETIC MAGICK FOR LUCKY LOVE

Luck in love can be achieved in several ways. If you look at the list of stones in a previous chapter, you will find several for luck. You simply would carry them unless I put other directions.

You can carry lucky flowers, plants or herbs. Such as a Four Leaf Clover, Bay Leaf, Cinnamon or Lotus Flower.

Sympathetic Magic is when you use or carry something that represents your intent. Remember: Like attracts Like. The astral forces will connect the item to the person/situation.

If your intent/purpose is to have luck in meeting someone new for a romantic relationship, you can do the following, as an example:

Get a white image candle, a pink or white Seven Day candle or a candle of any size.

With green ink or paint, draw the outline of two people on it holding hands and put a smile on each face. (They can be stick figures.) The green will bring lucky love vibrations.

Light the candle on a Friday or Sunday at any time. Focus your intent as you light it for a minute or two. At this point you don't have to stay, but leave the candle burning.

Let the candle burn down to the socket. Do not put it out.

When it is done, anything that might remain at the bottom has to be thrown away outside of your home.

HEX-BREAKING

SOMETIMES there are those who wish us not to do well. This could take the form of a spell, cast out of jealousy, with subconscious or conscious intent. It could be a toxic relationship that still persists on some level. Whatever the reason, it can slow down our intent or cancel it altogether.

We achieve our goals or not (if it isn't good for us) upon our own merit. We can't have others interfering in our lives in a negative way. We are not going to give them that personal power. We will be dynamic about moving forward.

There are things that we can do to cancel these situations out. Remember that sometimes it isn't a curse, just the wrong timing or just something we work on that's not good for us. If it is not caused by a curse, hex or negative thought, what we do to cancel it out will simply keep going to the ethers and dissipate. It cannot harm.

There are several modalities that you can utilize. Here are a few:

1 - Take a cross or whatever connects to your belief system or a picture of it and hang it above your door/doors coming into your home.

2 - Take the herb called rosemary and burn it in your home to rid it of all negative influences. It cleanses and purifies the energies in your home. If you place some under your bed, it keeps you from harm. It is a good substitute for Frankincense.

3 - Wearing the stone called the Tiger Eye not only protects you but is a boomerang and sends back negativity to anyone sending it to you. Never name a person because it might be someone else or more than one person. It will not do serious damage to whoever sent the hex to you. We are Light Workers, Wizards of Light and Magi. We work with the Light and in the Light.

4 – Carry these herbs by themselves or combine them. It is best to carry them in a pouch/bag/medicine bag/mojo bag/handkerchief or whatever is convenient. The best pouch color is white or purple. Herbs: Rosemary, Mint, Bergamot, Geranium or/and Vetivert.

5 – Oils vibrate as magnets. The best essential oils are Sandalwood, Uncrossing, Success or Geranium. You can mix it in a bottle containing some olive oil to make more. Place a drop on your pointer finger or thumb and touch your Third Eye (middle of your forehead), throat, heart, bottom of feet and center of your palms. These are energy centers. Pray for protection to Divine Power or your deity. Do this every day upon awakening in the morning and upon going to bed at night.

MYSTICAL FORCES

THERE are spiritual forces behind symbols and talismans. Knowing what they are and how to work with them gives us a jumpstart to do better in our lives.

Symbols can come in various forms, such as seeing an answer in the clouds, in the flight of birds (birds flying toward you represent information coming to you, birds flying away mean you are meant to give out information/advice or some form of communication to someone), the way stones fall, pictures in the dirt on the ground, in trees, cards, runes and other forms for psychic or occult/paranormal information.

Talismans are consecrated objects to attract your intent, protect you, and for banishing negative energies around you. Any purpose you can think of, there is a talisman. (Or we make them up specifically for you.)

So let's use a few.

CARD MAGNETS

The regular playing cards originated from the tarot cards. They are the Lower Arcana.

You can use the playing cards in several ways. You can carry them. You can also make a copy of them, fold them and carry them. The vibration will be the same, but copy them in color, not back and white.

You can also place them on your bed between your mattress and box springs or on a nightstand. Or you can place it with the picture on the card facing you behind a mirror.

These are the best cards:

The Ace of Hearts = Happiness, love in all forms, and contentment.

The 7 of Hearts = Love and marriage.

The 3 of Hearts = Celebration, joy, fun.

LAW OF LOVE

This is one of the Laws of Nature/Spiritual Law. It states that, like Karma, what we put out in love/friendship comes back to us threefold.

If someone is a mean person, he/she will attract the same basic type of person until he/she changes. Someone loving and warm and positive will not feel comfortable around such a person. Think about how you feel around someone critical, mean-hearted, or disapproving. It is not the loving, supportive energy that you want to be around.

To attract certain traits in the one you want as a lover, marriage, romantic relationship or friend, you need to develop those traits in yourself.

If you want someone warm, you can't be cold. They are opposite energies and will not mesh for long. If you are looking for a loyal friend, you need to also be that. If you should look for someone giving, you cannot be a miser. If it is communication you search for, you need to be communicative. Don't confuse communication with agreeing. If you disagree in a conversation, you are still communicating.

OMENS

Omens are signs signaling the coming of an event.

Magi, shamans, psychics, intuitive/sensitive people, Kahunas and other spiritual people have always looked for and recognized omens. It does take practice and awareness.

Client's Story:

One of my clients for several years noticed that every time a new romantic relationship was coming into his life, he would get a minor headache that didn't go away for a few days and then he'd meet the new person. The headaches weren't painful as much as they were annoying. Once he recognized the omen/pattern, he would know when someone new was coming and would get ready. He would straighten up his apartment, put food in the refrigerator, buy wine and in general get ready for his new relationship.

You might have an omen too. Consider, when you began a new relationship or met a new friend, what happened first. Sometimes it's simply a matter of you always deciding that you are meeting someone NOW. Or you see butterflies everywhere, as on the TV, outside, pictures.

If you don't have an omen or can't spot it, ask, with reverence, respect and sincerity, for the universe to give you a sign whenever you (fill in your intent) and specify what you want as a sign and that you recognize it. Otherwise you may not know it when it happens.

SPIRITUAL LINKS (+ and -)

Have you ever met someone in your past who you still feel connected to? You may think of the person out of the blue ten years later and wonder what they're doing. They are most likely thinking strongly of you and that's what you sensed/picked up.

Or you feel like there's a connection but don't understand it. Someone who you have a strong pull to think of, for example. That doesn't mean you aren't happy in your life or even that you ever want to see the person, but there's a definite link spiritually.

It could be caused by a past life connection or the connection you built in this one. You might have had a very emotionally intense sensual/sexual/loving relationship and for some reason it didn't work out.

You both created a spiritual link. Think of it as an umbilical cord of white or one with blue and white light connecting you. Normally this is positive and will give you a reminiscing feeling. You might remember warm feelings or wonder what the other person is doing now or simply wonder why you are feeling or thinking about the person.

If it was a negative experience that was emotionally upsetting, you want to break that link once and for all. This is how:

1 – Draw the first picture (can be stick figures) of you and the other person facing each other at a small distance with a white light umbilical cord connecting you.

2 – Next, think of a gigantic sharp tool that's made completely out of Pink Light that cuts. (Pink is universal love energy.) Scissor, knife or something else (I had a client who thought of a machete).

3 – Draw the second picture of both of you still facing each other and connected with the umbilical cord. Then draw the gigantic cutting tool in Pink Light cutting through the cord.

4 – In your third and last picture, draw a picture of both of you facing away from each other (backs facing toward one another) and draw a smile on both faces! Focus on both of you walking away from each other, both of you walking toward your Highest Good.

5 – Then burn the paper to ashes. You might have to relight it until all of it turns to ashes. Then take it outside and throw it to the wind and forget about it. You broke the link and will think of the person less and less through time. That is simply now your memory, not the strong pull of the link.

CUPID

You can "call in"/"summon" a deity to your aid. First, do your own form of protection or use mine:

<u>Say the Prayer</u> with verbal conviction and command. The more you expect, the more that comes in.

Protection Prayer

I, <u>(say your name)</u>, now call on Archangel Michael, (or use your own deity connection)

Hear me as I call on thee! I decree that thou protect my mind, body and soul. Hear me, oh great and powerful Archangel of Protection. I command thee thus to come to me now. I am Radiant Light housed in my physical body. Protect me until this work is done. Thank you.

So Be It!

Next, call on Cupid. Even though this is a positive deity, you are opening a portal when you call and you don't want anything negative hitchhiking or sneaking in through the portal. That's why we always do Protection first.

<u>Say:</u>

Cupid, Cupid, hear my plea,

Bring my new love unto me,

With speed of flight,

With strong desire,

I now await with heart of fire.

Thank you and go forth until this is done. So Be It

Go about your daily business, knowing that your new love is coming to you. Cupid is sprinkling love energy all around you. Take a chance when it comes in.

HEALING YOUR PAIN TO MOVE FORWARD IN LOVE/FRIENDSHIP

Sometimes we've been hurt so much in our past that it's difficult to move on to a new relationship. If your guard is up all the time (for good reason), others perceive that as a sign that you don't want to be bothered by them and you might miss out on a wonderful relationship.

Are you really open and ready for love or do you have barriers (conscious or not) that still delay it?

This old technique helps to forgive yourself, release blocks that keep you from your joy, gives balance, peace, freedom and love. This technique brings emotional, physical and mental balance.

This is a Mantra. You repeat it for a few minutes at a time or as long as you feel you should continue. You are planting a spiritual seed. Do this each day until you feel a sense of being released.

<u>Say:</u>

I am sorry

Please forgive me

Thank you,

I love you.

Meaning: I am sorry (for being part of this incorrect past action)

Please forgive me (for replaying old memories that are no longer valid and not seeing the perfection of the here and now)

Thank you (for cleansing me and the universe)

I love you (the Divine, also in me and others. I see my mistakes as being a human trait and now they can be cancelled)

You have so much to look forward to. You are breaking patterns. All those possibilities, opportunities, new love, new friends to meet. Open your heart and let them in. You have a lot to offer. Dream big and go for it by taking action. I have faith in you. You are transmuting.

NEW LOVE

First, don't close doors. Emotionally or otherwise.

<u>Men</u> – If you ask someone out and they say they can't go, ask if there's a better time for them. Sometimes there's a good reason. If you get turned down, it is their loss. They don't know what magickal happenings there could've been and they were the wrong person for you, so you dodged a bullet now instead of discovering your incompatibility after many dates.

Move on to better experiences. What was that about kissing a lot of (lady) frogs first?

Women – If someone asks you out and you would like to go but can't at that day, don't just say no. It closes a door and it will be taken to mean you don't want to go out – ever. Simply say: *I can't go out on (   ), but I can go on (_____).*

No closing doors here . . . Setbacks help you meet the right person instead. They spark your energy to get out there more.

A GINSENG FORMULA FOR A NEW LOVE

This plant is under the planet energy of the Sun and its element is fire. Need I say more? It is used for new love and lust.

Take a ginseng root, and, holding it between your hands, energize it by putting your focus into it for your outcome. Carry it at all times to attract new love and for sexual potency. It is said that if you drink a tea of ginseng, it is a powerful lust-inducing tea by itself or mixed with other similar herbs.

HERBAL SPELL CASTING

Herbs can be traced back to ancient rituals and formulae. They are vibrationally attracting in various, almost unlimited, situations. They have more than one purpose. We are looking at a few for the purposes of love, lust and friendship.

Star Anise – Burn for luck in your endeavors. You can also place it in a bucket with water. Let it sit for 20 minutes and use it as a floor wash.

Cloves – Used in ritual magick in seeking to aid love or begin love or/and friendship.

<u>High John</u> – Used in several ways, one of which is in great love spells.

<u>Whole Vanilla Bean</u> – Used as an aphrodisiac. For centuries it has been known to stir your senses. It also helps to stir love and desire. Carry it and put a piece into a spiritual bath.

<u>Orris root</u> – Used in bringing good luck to love affairs, passion and marriage. To find and hold love, carry the root. Or use as powder in a pouch.

<u>Rose</u> – Emotional balance, harmony, family, love and success in these. Wear performing love spells. Put one on your altar for love.

<u>Strawberry</u> – Connected to planet Venus and the deity Freya. Serve these as love food.

HERBAL LOVE MAGICK

The herb to be used in this formula is called Patchouli. You work with it to attract love and passion.

It is best to work with Patchouli on a Sunday (this herb is connected to sun energy).

This herb will attract women and men alike. To use, wear this herb with other love herbs or by itself.

You can also get Patchouli in oil form. In that case, you would put a drop or two on your palms, wrist and heart.

MAGICKAL FRIENDSHIP

The flower we utilize here is Gardenia. It has several uses, such as love, passion and, of course, friendship.

Wear this flower to attract friends that are new. You can also get the essential oil and wear that on your palms, wrist and heart. Only a few drops are needed.

GARDENIA LOVE MAGNET

This formula is to be done by the light of the moon. (Any moon phase will do.)

Dry the petals of the flower. When dry, crush them in a container where you can add another herb.

Mix ground Orris Root with the Gardenia.

To attract your opposite sex, lightly dust your body with this blend.

GREEN SPINE LOVE

The above is simply another name for the herb called Spearmint.

The best time to work with this formula is when you are outside and it's a little windy.

Use Spearmint when adding it to any love mixtures or carry it in a white or red pouch.

YOU ARE NEVER ALONE

YOU are not alone. You are living in a universe that's abundant in everything, including love, friends, family, and, of course, lust.

There are always people around you. Smile (you're more approachable) and talk to people, even if it's on a supermarket line.

Look at your past relationships. I mean, really look. With each new person/situation, it gets better and better in some way. You are working your Path towards improving your life and happiness (which, remember, you deserve).

At this point, looking back, you should notice if you have a pattern. If that pattern is positive, that's great. If it isn't positive for you, with emotional strength and command, <u>say:</u>

All that is blocking and stopping me from my positive relationships is NOW removed, sent back to the universe to transmute it to good and bring the right relationship back to me. It Is So!!

Divine Intervention has to fully fill the gap that's in your life for whatever is your intent, so it can make things better. Focus on your purpose and what you're manifesting emotionally and/or physically. Then keep an eye out and pay attention to your surroundings/situation and expect it to come. It does.

YOUR HEART'S DESIRE

This will take a little time, depending on each person's motivation and clear thoughts. Follow the <u>directions to achieve your intent:</u>

You will need: white paper, black ink, something to burn the paper in (can be a cauldron or ashtray or anything that works for you) and matches.

Write on white paper with black ink at the top:

1 -THIS OR BETTER

2- IN A PERFECT WAY

3- FOR THE GOOD OF ALL

Now, write the positive qualities of all your past relationships that connect to your intent (love, romantic love/lust, family, etc.). Also think of positive qualities you've seen in other people that you like and add those to your list.

Review your list and add anything you're missing.

Focus on your intent as you reread the list.

Get excited about it.

Place the list in your container so that you can burn it.

With your intent being strong and with conviction, light the paper, and <u>say</u>:

Lords of Love and Lords of Fire,

Bring to me what I desire,

From dusk to dawn,

From dawn to dusk,

I open my heart,

I know I must.

And So Be It!

After all the paper has burned (you might have to relight it), throw the ashes to the wind. Let it go emotionally and don't focus on it anymore so the Lords can work on it and bring the results to you.

THE POWER OF THE WORD

WORDS have power and we as shamans, spiritual leaders, magi, prophets, masters, occultists and people in other similar fields have utilized this power since ancient times.

Words of power are meant to be spoken out loud and with command.

Think of what you are manifesting into your life, what you are looking for, what are your goals? Then, when you use any of these words or whatever word fits your intent, make them into sentences. Such as:

I now manifest a positive romantic relationship with someone who is (fill in). So Be It!

Some of these words can be spoken on and off when you are working on manifesting your intent:

Love, intelligence, communication, monogamy, harmony, balance, sexual, sensual, romantic, honest, trust, fun, humor, happy, healthy, warm, compatible, respectful, emotionally supportive, adventurous, travels, hugs, considerate and any other qualities you are looking for.

*** Remember, before you start to also be conscious of what YOU are PUTTING INTO the relationship. It cannot be one-sided. There is a balance in nature. ***

VENUS OF LOVE

Venus is a Love Goddess. We can call on her to come to our aid to attract the right love/person to us.

Wear something green. It is best to do this ritual on a Friday.

And, with reverence, say three times:

Venus, Venus come to me,

Show me who I'm meant to be,

Send my true love right to me,

And as my will so mote it be!

OPEN HEART MEDITATION

Do this meditation in a quiet place where you will not be disturbed. Shut off any sound devices, like a phone, if you are indoors.

Sit comfortably. If in a chair, it's best to have one with arms so your body isn't focusing on whether you are falling over or not. Wouldn't that ruin the meditation?

You can read through it a few times, so that, when you meditate, you are not reading it. You will remember the basics. Or you can read it verbally into a recorder and play it back for yourself.

Take three deep breaths slowly with your eyes closed before you begin.

<u>Open Heart Meditation:</u>

See yourself in front of a door. Pay attention to all the details, such as: What material is it made of? What color is it? What type of handle or doorknob? What is the height?

Now, open the door and step inside to a beautiful, pristine mountainside. A sky that's blue. With lush green grass and tall trees with colorful leaves waving in the warm breeze. There are all types of colorful flowers. Look and see what the main colors are on the flowers.

Now you notice that you are stranding on a path. Again, become aware of the type of path. Is it dirt, brick, cement or something else? This path leads to a spot overlooking a broad, open valley with the same type of trees and flowers as the mountain you are on.

Walk on the path until you get to a point where you can comfortably have an overview of this beautiful valley.

Stand there for a few seconds and look around. Now, stand with your feet apart about shoulder width and both of your hands crossed in front of you over your heart. Stand like this and focus on your heart being closed and see that your hands are protecting it.

Take three deep breaths and open your arms upward toward the sky. It will look like you are standing with your arms heavenward in a "V" shape. Know that your heart is safe, that Divine Power always takes care of you and keeps you surrounded and permeated with love. Feel a soft warm breeze caressing you as if to say you are loved and hugged.

Shamans, Oracles and other Spiritual Leaders use this pose.

If you compare your arms forming the "V," it looks partly like you are standing in the "Victory" pose. Think of athletes who won a trophy, someone who accomplished and finished a task, or even children when they win (they will jump up and down in that stance, with their arms raised high).

You are victorious in love in all forms. Anything negative from your past is gone, never to return. Your heart is open, you are happy, safe, and are letting love come to you.

Put your arms down to your sides. Take a deep breath and turn on the path to walk back to where you started.

Notice the trees, flowers and your beautiful surroundings.

Stand in front of your door; take one last look around, feeling happy, joyous, free, and with an open heart.

Open the door and step through it.

Remember you can always come back to this spot at any time.

Take a deep breath and slowly . . . open your eyes.

LOVE INCENSE

Incense is a spell enhancer. Even though incense can be used by itself, you would usually use it with other tools, medicine bags, on an altar or other modalities, as part of a ritual or formula.

Whether used by itself or with rituals/formulae, incenses work vibrationally. Some of the incenses you can use to get you started for your intent are:

Love incense (of course)   Rose

Gardenia   Pine

Patchouli   Honeysuckle

FAERIE CIRCLE TO BRING SOMEONE BACK

FIND an area outside that seems a little private. Such as: a quiet corner in your yard, a spot at the base of a tree in the park, and so forth.

Love magick is private and personal, so do not talk about it to anyone until it comes to pass.

First, gather all your ingredients. You will need the following:

1 – These herbs, in any form – Two Roses (or petals), Two Orris Roots, and one Cinnamon Stick

2 – Patchouli Oil or Rose Oil

3 – Patchouli Incense or Rose Incense *** Use the same oil and incense scent so vibrations mesh. *** And something to burn it in.

4 – Stone – Rhodocrosite, Moonstone, a Pink Agate or Rose Quartz The size doesn't matter. A smaller stone will be easier to carry with you.

Put a drop of oil on the one stone you picked focusing on your intent for love.

Now, stand in the middle of the circle you will form.

Place the herbs going in a clockwise direction to form a circle around you. It doesn't have to be a large circle. The space between them doesn't matter because you are still forming a circle. Focus on energy flowing from one herb to another until you are back at the same spot where you started.

Place the incense and the stone in the center next to you.

Light the incense and with focus and reverence, <u>say:</u>

> *Faeries of the deepest deep,*
>
> *Bring my true love back to me,*
>
> *With open heart I wait and seek,*
>
> *Your Blessings if it's meant for me.*
>
> *Thank you.*

Stay in the center until the incense burns out. And stay focused on your intent. Important: During this time, send love energy to the fairies as payment for their work.

When done, take the stone to carry with you. Take the herbs and incense remains and throw them to the wind.

Walk away and don't look back.

THE ONE THAT GOT AWAY

WE often hear stories about "the one that got away." Sometimes it is a fish tale about the "big one," but mostly it is about that one special person that you crossed paths with during your sojourn of life, and, for whatever reason, you have lost touch with him or her but you think about them constantly.

Was it "true" love or was it merely a lingering lust? It might be both and that is perfectly normal. Lust may manifest as either physical or chemical attraction, or emotional, resulting from love. What do I mean by chemical? Have you ever seen two people together and felt you could almost sense/feel the physical attraction between them? Some call this "chemistry." The couple is a natural fit. As right as this may seem, the rational, conscious mind takes over, and we find several reasons why that couple should not be together. This is important to understand, as manmade law teaches us that Lust is bad and Love is good. Love, as we have seen, can also be bad and can take on many bad outward manifestations as well, including control, manipulation and abuse.

It is hard for many to agree that love and lust can coexist. You can love your husband or wife and lust after them as easily as you can love and lust after someone else. Think of love and lust as vibrational states of a soul connection. The beauty of manifestation is that we can touch the material form of our ethereal selves. If there is a soul connection based on karmic resonance – you both vibrate at the same frequency, so there is a comfort to the connection – and then that connection may form feelings on this plane as that energy is transmuted into emotions we understand. In other words, our spiritual connection manifests into love and/or lust.

That feeling you have of him/her "getting away" is a sense of physical loss, not spiritual. The connection is actually always there. Spiritually, we are always connected. There is no separation between spirit and physical. Our subjective consciousness tells us we are separated due to our perceptions of time and space. In reality, we are all connected. Have you ever thought of someone and they called a few minute later? That is not a coincidence. Even more amazing, but unknown, is that when you think of that person, chances are very high that they also just thought of you and vice versa. If you find yourself thinking of that special someone, the one that got away, suddenly and for no reason, they may have just thought of you.

Maya Angelou, the famous author and poet, remarked "I've learned that people will forget what you said, people will forget what you did, but people will never forget how you made them feel." What feels like a loss is that that person made you feel a certain way. That feeling was so different than anything you've ever felt and you still crave it. This drives your lust.

Don't feel bad about it. Don't feel guilty about it. What if I called lust magnetism or gravity? Science teaches us that opposites attract. Metaphysics teaches us that like attracts like, given vibrational similarities. The gravitational pull of planets is widely understood and we easily accept that the moon's pull on the Earth is one of the reasons for the rising and falling of tides. I submit that the gravitational pull of another is no different. We call it "lust," which is the emotional response to physical beauty. If we were blind, the energy would be the same. The vibration of the person's voice would still resonate and "turn on" certain physical senses just as that special someone did when you spoke to them on the phone.

Love and Lust are linked. Understanding and appreciating that link will go a long way towards reconciling what appears to be conflicting emotions. Lust is physical and emotional, just like love. Some will say, "When I look at erotic pictures, I feel lust for the person in the picture." In this case, what you are manifesting is a desire to be with someone you find attractive. Why is that bad? If you take that desire and manifest it as malformed intention – stalking or obsession – that is a misuse of the energy. Appreciating a physically attractive form and even thinking about being with that person is human and natural. It is not dirty and bad.

Lust's partner, Love, is there in duality as all other energies exist in the universe. All energy is dual, and by duality I do not mean good and evil. I mean dual as in a "balancing." Our subjective consciousness has been taught that if something is good, the other side must be bad. I prefer to think of duality as balance or counterweight. Without this counterweight, we would not understand the other, and vice versa. Like Yin and Yang, we understand the one by understanding the other. So, too, we understand Love by experiencing Lust, and Lust by experiencing Love.

CONCLUSION

LOVE is the language and force of the universe. When dealing with animals, you can easily observe their reaction to love. It has also been scientifically tested (as if we didn't know already) that plants respond to love, harmonious music, stress and other emotions.

Looking for love and lust, as well as improving the relationships and friendships we have, are very important in our lives.

I make medicine bags and talismans upon request for individuals, but without a true heart and intent it slows or cancels the magick. Your energies also need to have a frequency connection with your intent. Remember, "Like attracts Like." So, even on your own, be true to your heart's desires.

You now have the tools. Remember, the application of your knowledge brings results.

In finding ourselves we also find love.

Use these spiritual tools and allow love to come to you. Lust can give balance of the emotional and physical planes. We are, after all, spiritual beings in a physical body. While the friendships that we gain can keep us happy and young at heart.

You can utilize the information in my book to help you on your adventurous journey into a better life. Be positive. Go forward with joy, an open heart, excitement and let your love light shine for all to see.

YES YOU CAN!!!

80

MARIA D'ANDREA TELLS YOU HOW TO SEE THE FUTURE AND CAST SPELLS WITH AN ORDINARY DECK OF PLAYING CARDS

NOW YOU CAN GO BEYOND CARD GAMES OF MERE "CHANCE" AND INTO THE INFINITE!

The origin of playing cards is shrouded in the mists of time. Some historians trace them to the ancient Egyptians, others to the Chinese or medieval Italy, still others to the Romany gypsies seen so often in pop culture portrayals of fortune tellers. Wherever they come from, an ordinary deck of 52 playing cards are not mere "playthings" but are instead a mystical link to the great unknown. Anyone can master their use with diligent practice –and being born with supernatural powers is not required!

Learn how individual cards are like living entities with personalities and traits all their own. The king of clubs, for example, is humane, upright and affectionate, while the king of diamonds is continually fuming in his stubborn, vengeful wrath. The cards form a cast of characters enacting a drama that can give insight into your future and alert you to dangers you never previously imagined.

But one doesn't have to passively accept the fortune meted out by the seemingly "random" way the cards fall. Read Maria D'Andrea's spells involving the use of playing cards. She explains how the careful laying out of ordinary cards, when combined with the use of candles, incense and the recitation of ritual words, can make the "higher powers" do your bidding. You are in control of your future with Maria's methods and are not subject to the whims of unseen forces working through artful pieces of cardboard. This is a golden opportunity to gaze and control the future – from a perspective of self-determination – that you can't afford to miss!

Order your copy of SIMPLE SPELLS WITH PLAYING CARDS for only $22.00 + $5 S/H

* * * * *

ALSO AVAILABLE

GYPSY WITCH FORTUNE TELLING PLAYING CARDS – $12.00

Perfect for teaching yourself or others to use regular playing cards in your divination, the Gypsy Witch Fortune Telling Playing Cards include small descriptive meaning on each card's face. This has been a popular deck for decades. Says one user: "Some people say these cards are just for fun, but these cards are not a game. I've had done readings on myself and others, they've turned out to be at least 90% accurate, both good and bad."

IF YOU WANT TO LEARN MORE ABOUT THE OCCULT THESE BOOKS BY MARIA D' ANDREA WILL BE MOST HELPFUL TO YOU! EACH BOOK $22.00 OR ALL EIGHT TITLES THIS PAGE FOR $139.00 + $15.00 S/H

( ) SECRET MAGICAL ELIXIRS OF LIFE

( ) HEAVEN SENT MONEY SPELLS

( ) SECRET OCCULT GALLERY AND SPELL CASTING FORMULARY

( ) YOUR PERSONAL MEGA POWER SPELLS

( ) HOW TO ELIMINATE ANXIETY AND STRESS THROUGH THE OCCULT

( ) MYSTICAL AND MAGICAL BEASTS AND BEINGS

( ) OCCULT GRIMORIE AND MAGICAL FORMULARY

ALSO AVAILABLE — 10 Thirty Minute Workshops by Maria on DVD - $80

ORDER NOW FROM: TIMOTHY G. BECKLEY, BOX 753, NEW BRUNSWICK, NJ 08903

32380252R00047

Made in the USA
Middletown, DE
02 June 2016